BONE SKID,
BONE BEAUTY

SAINT JULIAN PRESS

POETRY

Praise for *Bone Skid, Bone Beauty*

To read Jane Creighton's poems is to be held, gratefully, in what she calls "the glinty vise of memory." We slide with her in and out of dreams, walk the ragged edge of old loss and fresh, vivid connection with the natural world and a touching variety of people, some known, some strangers. *Bone Skid, Bone Beauty* (starting with its magical title) is intense and beautifully wrought, its reach wide and deep. It's only a shame that it's taken so long to be given to us.

—Rosellen Brown, author of *The Lake on Fire*
Cora Fry's Pillow Book, *Half a Heart*, and *Before and After*

In *Bone Skid, Bone Beauty*, Jane Creighton gives us the marvels of poetry as it moves between dreams and memories, salt and mist. Reading her renews our claim on the beautiful nature of those elemental tools an artist uses to shape meaning with words. And what meaning she makes: exhilarating and devastating. I am reminded of Virginia Woolf's phrase in the opening lines of *Mrs. Dalloway*: "what a lark, what a plunge." Great pleasure can be found in the cadences and musicality of Creighton's lines, in the perfect fit of idea and image; also, there is great surprise and pain in being taken down into the intimacies of grief. This work is motivated overall by what the unsettling presence of the dead signifies for the living. In this time of plague and incalculable loss, Creighton's poems offer necessary guidance for nurturing the ghosts of 2020 and cultivating the gardens of 2021. So many memorable and quotable lines, I leave you with one, a description of poetry itself: "The door unlocks itself and opens / Into a field crusted with the spiny tips / of words."

—Kay Turner, author of *Beautiful Necessity:*
The Art and Meaning of Women's Altars,
and *What a Witch: The Wise Woman*
in Folklore, History, and Performance

It takes a certain patience, the will to endure, to make language sharp enough to slice through time. Jane Creighton's *Bone Skid, Bone Beauty* patiently observes a world surrendering the past to an ever- mobile "now." There, Lot's Wife and Orpheus serve not as figures of regret but as gatherers of wisdom in crisis, who "Salt the wet horizon / with thimbles full of stories: / what we did, where we went, / what we want back, even as / the city burns." Nowhere is this mediation on the persistence of place and the ghosts of memory more powerfully jagged than in the sonnet crown "Weight and Measure." There Creighton unveils the past full of "blurred figures piloting a floating mist," a past where "So many stories / flicker at the edge, / softening the quick blow, / the regret." *Bone Skid, Bone Beauty* musters the will to see the world as it is without fashionable malaise or facile hope and to reside in a radiant now, where it is "as if / we had all, always been friends / who loved one another / in the same place, at the same time." *Bones Skid, Bone Beauty* lives at that very place and time.

—Joseph Campana, author of
The Book of Life, *The Book of Faces,* and *Natural Selection*

BONE SKID, BONE BEAUTY

Poems

by

Jane Creighton

SAINT JULIAN PRESS
HOUSTON

Published by
SAINT JULIAN PRESS, Inc.
2053 Cortlandt, Suite 200
Houston, Texas 77008

www.saintjulianpress.com

ISBN-13: 978-1-955194-00-6

Library of Congress Control Number: 2021936728

Cover Design & Author Photo Credit: Angel Quesada
Photo of *Florisphaera profunda* by Alicia Kahn
Inside Visual Art Images: Alicia Kahn & Angel Quesada

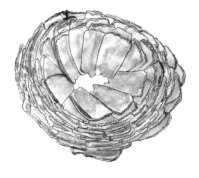

FOR BROTHER

It is like what we imagine knowledge to be:
dark, salt, clear, moving, utterly free,
drawn from the cold hard mouth
of the world, derived from the rocky breasts
forever, flowing and drawn, and since
our knowledge is historical, flowing, and flown.

—Elizabeth Bishop
from "At the Fishhouses"

TABLE OF CONTENTS

Adequate Proof of Land   1

I

Salt and Mist   4
Weight and Measure   5
Her Best Wish   12
You Show Up   13
Cy Twombly in the Thicket of Light   14
Standing in Gallery 8   15

II

Moment   18
Sequence from the Back Yard   19
Lake Dreams, Annaghmakerrig   22
Bone Skid, Bone Beauty   27
The Trees on Prairie Road   30
Where There Is No Else   31
People   32
Planning for Time   34

III

Standing Mirror   36
Lake Dreams, Blue Mountain   38
My Mother in the Void   45
Weird Little Prairie   46
Far West Texas   47
Monosyllables   48
The Afternoon Is the Medium   49
The Woman You Once Will Be   50

IV

Absence at Dusk 52
Word Count: Sidewalk, Long Beach, Café Table 53
Soul to Take 56
What We Said About Limits 57
This Way of Being Here 58
Before. After. 59
Late August from a Dead Stop 60
The Visit 61
Slumber 63

V

My Village 66
Ping Shan Heritage Trail, Hong Kong 67
Friday Morning 68
A Figure 69
When Brother Reckons 70
Virus Days, April 71
Inside the Loop 81
July Ides / A Ghazal 84
Here and There 85
Supplicant 86

BONE SKID,
BONE BEAUTY

Adequate Proof of Land

Beyond the yellow-lit blue horizon
in the child's book about Noah's Ark, a bird
bears the leafing twig of an olive tree
along with the certain knowledge, although
the child didn't think about this, that olives
grow on trees. But she didn't eat olives
at that time, so that proof escaped her.

In other words, she had only faith
that land lay out there beyond the water
and she had it because she liked
how pretty the drawing was, how much
the blues carried light, as if
in a simple drawing of the ocean
a child might find her beating heart.

I

Salt and Mist

Lot's wife, sure.
Looking back. Punished
for paying attention to all
that mattered, all that was left
behind in the mad, flung forwardness
of escape. That's

what we sometimes do.
Salt the wet horizon
with thimbles full of stories:
what we did, where we went,
what we want back, even as
the city burns.

Weight and Measure

1.

It could have gone the other way. I could
have said, "I'll have this baby," lifted up
those heavy breasts—a song to life—and stood
to thicken in the heat, cursed and cupped
the pleasing turn of body into bearer
and helped myself to more of what I thought
my mother bore. So now some mornings rarer
than the moon's fertile trace, I plot
elusive breath, a syllable, bare wit
and other things it might have said, its voice
skittery in breaking light, the kid
who'd mirror me, or not. Alert or coy.
I might have had a daughter, or a son.
I might have run my mother's race, and won.

2.

I might have run my mother's race and won.
A skip and a hop, twelve steps to the corner
and back, twisting her skirt, it was fun
to kick heels in a rainy wind, faster
than the fat drops splattering her blue pumps
as she walked on inside. I waited
it out, feathering the front porch steps
with a dance I knew to make the rain
keep going. All this faintly rendered, so much
to remember. The sky slate grey, the grass
scented with thunder, too green to touch,
or touching, to stay and hold as waves passed
through me. How I would let one go for another,
how I would race inside to find my mother.

3.

How I would race inside to find my mother.
Tell about the strange dog heavy
by the bush. A toad! The king snake slithering
across my toes. I stood still, a breath
of lilac settling the maze of stark grief
that snake startled into life, my life. Huge,
Mama, the tail that went into the leaves.
She never stopped her work, pressing a blue
shirt, whoosh of steam, the iron's clunk
as she set it down, smiled at me and folded
my trailing fear like winter wool into a trunk
so that the summer light returned. I hold
one thought, then another, an easy turn
from water-bearing vessel to an urn.

4.

From water-bearing vessel to an urn,
they joke, using rougher terms for life
and death, the same-old, same-old; a yelping cur
scuttling the periphery, rolls its bleary eyes
for a handout. Old men laughing. They stamp
their feet in a corner of my mind reserved
for them, dark-lit and huddling a lamp.
Thoroughly drenched, lusty and nameless in the surge
of storm I've mustered without much thought,
they shake their heads in spite of me, wise
with the task of making do with what they've got,
which is, a lodging place in the glinty vise
of memory. Are they something I once read?
They visit, whistling in the face of dread.

5.

They visit, whistling in the face of dread
but not too often. No use wasting
their fresh weight in a too familiar bed
made daily, its pillows plumped with dulling haste.
We wake, sometimes, to necessary measures.
Trot them out to still the occasional pain
of sunlight dappling the blinds. We think pleasure
lives somewhere else—down the way,
where a woman might, right now, be singing
to herself, mindless of the jagged round
of betting, the slow payoff, and the sting.
We forget the quick fall and startling leap,
the hope of rising from a troubled sleep.

6.

The hope of rising from a troubled sleep,
a close dream pitched to the bony turrets
of a body now like a fortress, besieged
and whirling, firing out. A slur
of time grizzles the faint light that lifts
me from that place, pales the bleeding dark
and gathers up the night's two-fisted
worry. What was it? A lost girl? Parked
and wailing in the broken earth, she'd flung
her hands—mine now—upward. That was the end.
How to manage, I wonder, the sharp tug
of that girl and her mother, or the old men
failing me. They drift away from this,
blurred figures piloting a floating mist.

7.

Blurred figures piloting a floating mist:
that so-and-so, she'd married up, remember?
The boy who caught you with a first kiss,
or the first one bedded that bleak October
in a hotel far from home? So many stories
flicker at the edge, softening the quick blow,
the regret. A mother, mothering, lost shores
found elsewhere, in a body that weathers slow-
breaking waves until it relents and forgives
what I have, and haven't, done. My watery voice
purls her long-dead accents, alive
in the daily parceling of this life, the choice
morsel, the will to say once, and say
only, it could have gone another way.

Her Best Wish

To keep her hands in the dirt
kneeling. All fours.

To plant her left cheek
right down there

on the topsoil, eye-
balling the place where

the radishes will plump
and fill. To stay there

without pain or thought
of anything other than this

whole little bit of earth
where everything happens,

sun, rain, night, day,
mist, a rolling fog, the unsettling

hope of spring corralled against
all that mess, all the rest

of the big world. Karen, there.
The earth in her hair.

You Show Up

In the lassitude
of an afternoon
in a pickle of thought
as a bright red

suitcase snapped open,
your furled contents a glorious
nestling of all I'll never
know about you, any

or all of you floating,
a measuring cup
of faces poured out
across daylight all

not quite remembered
so much as felt in this
account: one body seated
of an afternoon certainly

not early but not quite
late in life and she
is thinking. A sculpture,
in fact, of thought where

blankness grows a fringe

Cy Twombly in the Thicket of Light

—after *Analysis of the Rose as Sentimental Despair*
Menil Collection

All it takes is one solid word
for all to turn on a dime. *Russet,* for instance,
for bracing romance, as in russet hair
against pale skin lit by heavenly light
whose provenance, in the painting that rises
from this word, is unknown. Or russet potatoes
in a bouncing boil, almost ready
for black pepper, butter, and cheese. Which
hearty desire? And at what moment
does it carry the day in and day out
of our most perfect understanding?

All it takes is one liquid utterance
unending, untenable. *Rose,* for instance,
spiking the mobile heart, as in red light
parsing the aqueous white of desire
in the painting that rises from this word.
His flames are like water it manages to say,
which is to say, no beginning,
no satiate end to the life-giving sorrow
of a heart that hungers and thirsts and
lifts itself against the fatal outlines
of its most perfect understanding.

Standing in Gallery 8

—after Twombly's *Say Goodbye, Catullus,*
to the Shores of Asia Minor
Menil Collection

When Orpheus turned to look at her
it was the end of something and the beginning
of something else, a budding protest
turned mortal longing turned a failing so earnest so

back to back to back that it blossomed all
inside itself, suffocated, and collapsed.

A fragrant boil in the great white air.
a memory, a fragment of a human
being. Oh, we push and push
against everything we have to lose

and still, we love. Birdlike. Swift.
We dive the pitiless horizon

surprised, always, by the bright
return of progress toward our ends
and the tidy respite of tasks, our stories
like beds, made. Unmade. As when

Orpheus turned, the keening puzzle,
the paling air, and water swept
the desolate earth.

II

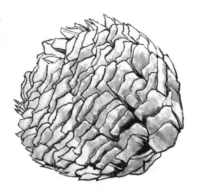

Moment

So always going going going walking riding
right behind Brother or just ahead of him on a trail

a sidewalk a mud bank along the creek the Honda
Trail 90 motor cycle bouncing the horizon of a cornfield

or walking with our sister from the hospital at 95th all
the way down to the East Village the spring morning

in 1969 when our mother's death punctuated who we were
and would be and what we would do / pavement slick

with fog or the just aftermath of what might have been
a night's rain, but we could not think of causation then

or consequence beyond three figures walking alone among
others others others in the streets of that city and this country

mighty and beleaguered, so if asked for a moment, this is
one of them following Brother and Brother following,

a sibling tag team and a dare.

Sequence from the Back Yard

1.

A heart pulsing strong enough
to beat back those little doubts
about this and that: a poorly planted shrub
a smile too faint, that thing I said once
that made my sister wince.

Flip it, then. Hold doubt like a slippery
heart, a little minnow darting the water
pooled in cupped hands, the precious
guest who can't decide if and when
and how she'll go.

2.

It is the cardinal more than anything
that draws us, no matter those sweet Texas doves
flocking the bird feeder, filling up all that green
actual springtime that I—a girl from four northern
seasons—never really believe exists until I hand myself
down into a life lived here, a back porch looking out,
the loved one happy in his chair, the cardinal
a blood-red streak sewing the line between us

3.

Cartoon bombs float by. A breeze
of hummingbirds mutes the wicked perimeter
where miscreants—those crafty finches—
haul away the Niger thistle. Once, twice,
and once more, a coyote came to visit. Solemn,
interested. No match, though, for the blue jays
and their birdy missiles. But this
is silly. The animals are friends, ours.
Why would I imagine a battlefield
in the backyard, flushed with spring,
where everything is up for grabs?

4.

Sunday

I doodle air with my big toe
and spin my chair, recalling
avuncular advice to quiet my hands
when I'm talking, stop twirling
that hair. All grown up now,
I salute the phantom
of my departed elders,
place these broad hands
flat on the table and thrum
a composition, a rhythm path
to draw them near.

5.

Cave lesson:

Use this nugget of air
to thwart. Today, good words
have fled. You may think
you'll follow them out, find light,
discover a water source,
but today you'll curl around yourself,
plowing darkness without seed.

Lake Dreams, Annaghmakerrig

1.

I had a father. He came home from work
to the sunny room, all about him
a family flushed with laughter, teasing.
We gave him what he wanted,
a plexiglass wall, its surface textured
in coarse little bumps over which he could run
his fingers. All it needed was to be bolted
to the room's far wall. Then he could sit for hours
touching it, watching the dull
whiteness stilled behind it.

We were thoughtful children. We used
skill beyond our strength to raise it,
our backs bent to the load. We crashed it
into place, the older ones holding it
while the younger climbed up their bodies
to fix the bolts at the top. How many of us
were there? How is it that we had no names?
I had a father. He came home from work.
We helped him find his way across the plush
carpet. Straddling the day bed, the plump duvet,
he leaned into the glass, spreading his arms.
I reached for him, but the horrible
white cat attacked. It had no teeth,
devoid of claws, yet hurled itself
in fury between me and this father,
this faintly murmuring father. There, there,
he said. There, there.

2.

He's in the hallway packing. He's fifty-three
if he's a day, but he's going to war again. Light drifts
from the outer windows, enough to see him
in the shadows, the matter-of-fact cinching
of a strap, the pause to choose a shirt,
his back turned toward me fleshy and pale
like a fish belly rolling up in dark water.

This must be thoughtless motion
a staring into blankness beyond which
the inexorable steps into daylight occur.
He will board the airplane, saddled up
amidst rows of anonymous others. Everything
will be silver-gray, punctuated by the opening
and closing of mouths, incidental things
they say to each other while the future
settles into their skin. A hot wind,
a little bit of Arabic thundering into the horizon
but he won't think of it, of how little
or how much he knows, nor will he wonder,
anymore, about home. There is only
this sorry purpose left, putting
one foot in front of the other.

3.

Though dead, he still directs the funeral. Always quiet,
he gets his way through suggestion, a gesture,
the tilt of his head. Before you know it
you find yourself scuttling down his path,
all business, ready to do whatever he says.

So here he is, skin and bones, his mouth
a toothless O, lifeless but for these last orders:
Put this box here. Arrange the folding chairs thus.
Those bowls of daffodils? Along the windowsill,
a hedge to natural light.
                              But as the place begins
to fill, he grows anxious and recedes
into the still air behind the Victorian couch
where no one ever goes. "Too many people,"
says the fading voice. "Get them out."

I walk the drafty house, its cavernous halls leading
to the great grassy room where people gather
under lamplight. Even though I own this house,
the ladies in big hats will not listen to me
when I say, politely, that they must leave.
Dark-suited men walk the aisles, darkly celebratory.
They lean into the ladies, whispering
about the deceased, what was his,
what they'll gather of it, as the last bit of sunlight
drains from the windows. They plant themselves
under the butter yellow lamps and grow
until I am a vagrant note
in their bellowing chorus.

4.

The executioner's table scissors in bald light, an X
where the condemned are strapped, all torso,
arms and legs, the head left to dangle. She views it
behind the plate glass, led by the guard who suggests,
though it isn't made clear, that these accommodations
are for some, and not for others. What has she done?

He ushers her along a corridor that falls away
into a field where, lately, haymaking has begun.
So lovely, the fenced fields, sheep dotting
the rolling hills, the altogether sense of life carried on.
A cow bellows in the distance and she thinks
of reasons—an errant calf, full udders, perhaps
the luck of grass, the pleasures of singing out
just to hear one's own, full-throated self
head up, then back down again to the certainty
of food, the ceaseless tug and crunch—

They walk single file along the road bordering
these pastures, she just ahead. She hears him
behind her, his heavy steps and coarse, rhythmic breath
driving her forward, though he says nothing.
She'll know when to stop, at the gated sidewalk
leading down to the whitewashed cottage where she'll find
another version of herself, haggard and pale, naked
in the doorway, looking out. For her crimes
she'll stand twinned, once at the gate coarsely breathing
and once at the door, gnawing the air
as she hands off to herself, one by one,
a growing line of stolid, purposeful men.

5.

No more than the sound of the trees,
the knowledge of light beyond the thin walls
cloistering these dreams, wakes her.

It had been Áine this time
hanging onto the branch of a tree that grew
just over the stone wall, its roots
clutching the crumbling edge of a precipice.
There had been travels, an argument,
someone thrusting himself out of a car,
slamming the door in mountainous
country, but it was impossible to tell
who he was. She had looked, then,
across a patch of field capping a desperate bluff
and seen Áine, her head thrown back and turning,
in the last instant before the branch broke, to look
at the dreamer across the field, her eyes pooled with fear
and last hopes that she could be saved.

In the thicket of night, the animals sleep
or hunt according to their kind, rolling
into the curve of the earth, gravely dreaming
until the swans drift across the lake
into the daylight just outside the window.

Bone Skid, Bone Beauty

1.

Kim at Faifoo Cafe cooks
Tom Yum soup made
with vegetables and herbs she
grows and picks herself, mostly.

Working magic in her kitchen
with knives and pots,
she comes out to serve
and talk, a marvel

of kindness and efficiency.
A snapshot of the Texas
coastal bend, her life surmised
under the sweat of eating hot soup

that stirs this summer flesh,
these summer bones. Hard town,
she says. So many dreams
die here. Standing over a work table

she slices up fabric for the neckties
she packs with polyvinyl acetate
and sells from the cafe, perfect for cooling
the necks of old people working

their summer gardens. I buy the one
with black bucking broncos on a red backdrop
and pay for my lunch, dropping coins in the jar
she taps to make sure I'm paying attention.

For a friend, she says, who can't pay her rent.

2.

Waves of laughter and doubt.
When I first look out the window,
the morning air seems
hopeless, ponderous, thick
with dull doings, a day where all
is certain, everything set in place.

All it takes—a sidestep into not knowing,
a belly full of radiant weeping just
down some road, an old blue house
where the curtains billow their intent
and the one who lives through everything
curls herself into the grinning light.

3.

The door unlocks itself and opens
into a field crusted with the spiny tips
of words. They are dug in,

half-mouthed, spittled. They unpitch
and rise, finally, when the rains let loose.
The jawbone creaks, stretches

on its hinge. The good dog
gets up from the cellar floor,
scrabbles toward the light

and barks its unvarnished hunger
to rake those words up. To run.

4.

In the shell game where the treasure
is the money you lose
in the switcheroo, you might

forgo looking for the pea, forgo
the confidence game. Forgo, too, that other story
involving a pea. You heard it

in your lovely childhood,
the bruised back the delicate princess earned
from sleeping her burdened sleep

in the fairy tale that warned you away
from caring for luxury and wealth. You didn't
want to be that whining princess, nor

did you want the trouble of being fooled
by hands that moved too fast on a street corner,
the one you sought out so that

you might see
what the big world
was like. Nice, you thought,

if a little risky.
What you wanted, then,
was to keep walking, turn

the corner, see what's next. And so
you have, and here you stand, tumbling years
in your palm. She taps the jar.

You pay attention. One strand braided
to another and the next. You catch hold,
let loose, catch hold, let loose, drop

the coins in the jar and head out.

The Trees on Prairie Road

The road sidles by under the oaks
hooking business 35 to the water and may
have come into being somewhere
in the nineteenth century after a hard-fought
tangle with coastal brush. The oaks,
they've been here longer.

It slows you down
to think about the obvious. The thirst
of trees, the dearth of fresh water. Some
thirty miles to your back, salinification
of the Aransas whooping crane habitat
is killing the blue crabs, killing, in turn,
a far too significant number of cranes,
and still there is that indeterminacy
about the manner of your own
death. Pondered, idly, in the shade

of trees that have been here longer
than all the knowledge and sensation
you've gathered in your life, as precious
to you as that is. Coastal prairie,
parceled land, plotted world.

Where There Is No Else
(Panna Maria and Cestohowa)

Maybe 200 miles inland of hot road
spinning by, cotton fields, bony cattle,
barren land spitting up dust. Two immaculate
churches of Polish origin rise up out of the prairie
amid rumbling trucks hauling cotton bales,
amid turkey buzzards, shuttered houses
paling in the sun. You can't say
you know what's going on. You're simply
taking an outing away from your month
at the coast. You wouldn't say
you understand what it means
to build a church that echoes the triumphs
and travails of centuries of life
in southern Poland out here in the great
crisscross of southwest conquest and migration,
Texas. You wonder how these Poles managed
the difference between Russian onslaughts,
the promise of spring and mesquite, rattlesnakes,
precious little water. Where is home
when one needs it? Where is the whistle
in the distance calling you back? Pulling faith,
this is the great beyond, the pick-up-
your-bed-and-walk, the road
where if you don't survive,
someone else does.

People

Not enough of them in these poems.
Always a random thought, or animal
or vegetable, or someone's elbow shove,
the sprint around the corner, gone.

Where do they go, these people?
Why will you not summon them?
Your hardworking colleagues
who are busy, even now, getting ready
for classes, or the ladies who do aerobics
at the pool, the paralyzed post-gunshot fellow
who strains to kick his feet but doesn't hesitate
to say hello in the thick of his effort
to stay meaningfully alive, which is
something you ought to think about
when you wonder what the point is,

or if there is one, as if you get to pronounce
on the matter. Especially when there's fishing
and shrimping and writing and mailing and
digging and wiring and building and reclaiming
overlooked structures from the ravages of time,
salvaging buildings and saving bodies
and families and ecosystems as well as hairdressing,
manicuring, dressing up before surgery. Or

the four young women on the Port Aransas ferry
who piled out of their S.U.V. in bikinis and strutted
the deck, sure of themselves but looking, all the same,
frail enough to burn under the riveted gaze
leveled at them by every one of us
who sat in our hot cars watching.

It's hard to tell about people, what good
they will try to do, or what ill. Or
what it feels like to be one of them,
to be captive, to be captor.

Planning for Time

Shall we go west? Can you find me
that rattlesnake I almost walked right into
because I was looking down, concentrating
too much on the one-two one-two of my feet
headed toward the Devil's River, water, respite,
the complete change of being that swimming holes
in the desert always offer? Or shall it be
the ditch, the intracoastal waterway, passing
tugs pushing barges, the pleasure boat Urchin
churning toward Espiritu Santo Bay, a little lift
in my heart every time you say it, even though
I know what it will mean for this Yankee girl:
bugs and heat and stinging jellyfish, superb
languor, occasional dustups, and renewed surprise
each time I forget that alligators swim
these salt waters? To live in it. Breathe
all in, out. To long for. Anticipate.
To hesitate in the not-quite-there-yet,
so that we have not too quickly
been there already.

III

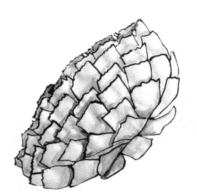

Standing Mirror

Spring again. So, I pitch a stone's
weight of restlessness into the flood,
standing naked on one foot. The mirror
jiggles and adjusts, mouthing the things I say:
Breast stroke. You. Move.
The knees bent, cracking, then sprung. I take

my own measure. Whatever works will take
time, like water lapping big stones
at Pleasure Beach where I clutched and moved
mountains of sand in my little bucket. A flood
sometimes. Where my rosy mother laughs, saying
Don't splash my glasses! Then exits the mirror.

I don't see any resemblance mirrored
in my hips, well, yes, they are solid. They take
up the space she left me when she left, saying
nothing I could hear across the stony
end-stop in her breath. A long pause. She floods
and recedes where I press flesh to glass, moving

myself along the edges of appearance, moved
by the stories I make for the mirror
how I dragged the dog half-drowned from the flood—
nope—that was my brother's childhood. I take
steps to be honest, as once stoned
on acid in the middle of Dorothy's saying

There's no place like home, heels clicking, I said
to the man next to me—his clothes restless and moving
about him too much like a stream shaping a stone—
I said Be quiet! It's true! Judy Garland mirrored
my young mother, more handsome than pretty. She took
offence at the likeness, so soon caught in the flood

of regretting her body, broad bright face flooded
with lost chances, she'd tell me. She'd say
don't stay but don't leave me. If I die, take
me home, bury me near water. I move
naked, one foot to the other. Mirror
exact motion from a body to a stone

rolled by a flood toward discrete moves,
my lips and mouth saying "no" to the mirror,
to the mother taking shape, and blood, and stone.

Lake Dreams, Blue Mountain

1.

A supple cat, black,
with scarlet panels running its flanks,
a gold flame coursing through them,
parades across an otherwise delicately
flat dream,
           wherein lake water laps
lake weed piling toward a grassy shore
and up from that, a house
closeted by trees.

I am in that house, walking
its dark corridors, one leading
to another, another, so that
I must ask:

          Am I circling?
          Have I seen this before?

And that is all. Only the cat
allows a slim moment where I might think
of purpose, the need to grasp and hold,
then it sidles off, flaming the darkness
and I walk out to the edge
a wordless waking in bent, hazy light

2.

You are to get on the bus,
keeping ankles and elbows
out of the aisle, eyes straight ahead
or, if you must, diagonally focused
toward a middle distance, a passing line
of tombstones, mossed and craggy
against a concrete sky.

This is a double-decker bus
too costly for the likes of you,
but we will let you on, won't even
take your money.
We have received our orders
to take you on a tour of this city.

There will be children running,
trying to get through the door,
but we will bat them away,
leave them with their hands open,
the thin lines of their bodies
rippling in the exhaust.

You have taught them to write, and
are likely to again because
instead of writing
they have taken to putting stones
in their mouths, and we wonder
what were you doing all that time?

Do not speak to the driver,
do not even notice him.
He has his job
and you have yours:

You are to look for the in-
between, borders and edges,
the postings between this life
and that, a woman hailing
a cab who calls forth, instead,
a storm of curses
from a frail and aging woman
who might be her mother

or yours, returned as a stranger
to remind you that no matter
how well you think you know
someone, chances are
she's holding something back.

Notice the black line of pavement,
the way she staggers across it,
spins into the periphery,
her hands, fingers, like darting
birds—here, then gone

while you, having followed our directions
most sincerely, sit motionless

and the bus hurtles forward
like a line you might have written,
spending its force in the dead ahead
of the sparkling and immense city,
its endless avenues
and withering grace.

3.

Benito, the husband, drives his cart toward a dark figure
who strikes the fallow field with a long staff.
The burro shivers its rump and Benito flicks the reins
as much at the flies as to drive it forward.
I shade myself in my rebozo under the slant rays
of a late sun and crouch behind him, watching
from the bed of the cart how the figure pitches
against the sky, like ink on a page of yellow light.

Am I Mexican? This must be Tejas,
a sweep of coastal land spreading
through the nineteenth century
toward the Rio Bravo, and the dark-figured man
has come to take it all away. I listen for the catch
in Benito's breath, a muttering that threads the air.

We have papers carefully folded
in the leather wallet I have made
for this purpose. I hold it in my hands.
Nuestra tierra, one of us whispers

in the limping Spanish the dream allows, so that
I am Mexican, only not. Beside myself
with posturing, with positing nothing
that will help Benito or myself rolling toward
that punctuating staff—
                              it parses the earth
just below the horizon, writing us
into a burning shadow, the dark figure flipping
the syllables of our names into the adumbrant lake
where she will dream us up as bit parts
in her sentimental epic, not knowing much
of anything, really. How I woke this morning,
arms wrapped tight around my body,
eyes opened to the near dark
before rising, bent to the task.

4.

How long have you had this power?

Since hightops.

That is the clue.
                    You are not
who I think you are, my spy partner,
a man so affable and generous that
during the hounding nights when we pursue
our craft, you'll sometimes pause in the thick
of edging around a dark corner, and ask,
So, how are you feeling?

Of course I won't answer. I'm a woman
in a man's job, proving my steeliness,
but grateful, and you know it

which gives you license
to lift a finger, make the windows shake.
I think about this before asking how—

Since hightops.
                    I can't
see you, am on the mezzanine.
Your words rise first, then spiky hair,
the fair falling slope of forehead,
eyes, nose, you!—your temperate mouth
smiling over the lip of the bamboo escalator
and in that instant no one but me

knows you are the harbinger
of an invading force. Kind
or malevolent, it doesn't matter. Either way,
I will have to change what I do,
the way I see my intent
in the mirror each morning

and I can't bear it. But neither
can I shout—you have frozen
my voice. My breath heaves
against the chords, until I break
into wakefulness, into evident night.

5.

I walk in the interregnum
between my brother and sister
tailing in their wake as they
move abreast into the city, each
with purpose, their arms working
the air, their legs pushing back
against the pavement in a stride
that makes the earth turn.

Like two independent states pressed
into peace along a festering border,
they glance sideways, then ahead,
marking each other's progress,
redoubling their resolve. They

have forgotten me, again.
They are older, they have
things to do. They have sublimated
hunger. But mine wails, a rocking,
fierce wave that I send crashing
against their backs, now! I need
to eat, now! But I'm the youngest,
and it's my dream, so no one
ever listens to me.

6.

Into the city
this one spilling its contents
across the drowsy end table,
flooding the floor, wall, window
until it sails itself out
into the night lake

Adrift amidst shifting, unstable towers
I wake myself, adjust my position
then fall back, fall back,
my head afloat on dislocated
faces mouthing their love,
their hate, their perfect
indifference.

My Mother in the Void

plays softball at first base,
catching a hit so fast and falling it
pocks her glove heading down,
takes her with it into the cobalt

infinity of the harbor that shifts, swells,
and evaporates in her daughter's mind.
So restless that mind is to hold her
before she slips away to what
she might have been at play.

Weird Little Prairie

By the sullen gate she stands on one leg,
barefooted, one foot lifted, a calf-scratch,
an itching wind. I call her up,
her testiness, her nervous desire, the way
she watches the far-flung road
and waits one more minute for something
to happen before she dares herself
into the country, stepping
into dust and dirt
to get herself out,
get away.

I sit in the chair in my office,
nearly sixty, trying
to get inside that picture,
some conjured, distant girl
running out her unknowns,
stepping it up, stepping forward,
no longer pausing
to catch her breath.

Far West Texas

More inspiring than you think
if you think only rolling waves
and the oily rot of marshes
harbor all that you could wish
of the surging, despotic shadows
that wake you up at night.

These are the thorny flats
of my most unarticulated wishes,
a dry and granulated yearning
for the buzz of light spindling
the ocotillo that waits for its
red blossom to burst
and punctuate the sky.

Monosyllables

Stones. Dirt. Trees.
Branch. Sand. Creek.
These feet. A boat. Hum.
And hum. Knock, roll,
fresh leads, clean
red sheets where
I might graze, hands
on the dream bell,
fits and starts,
a green pearl
and a moon, under
the tongue, wise.

The Afternoon Is the Medium

—after Aditi Machado's *Then*

Plumped in a chair, one book lap-settled,
several pages half-read and rustling as it

slips to the floor, you test time
by breathing. Whether nodded off

or awake matters little in the great scheme.
Try to remember this. Slide open

the sarcophagus lid. Stand upright
in the doorway. Flee the scene, dart

left or right in a game of shadows
or sit back down to the task to which

you have bent yourself, and it will still be
flesh raveling. It will still be breath.

The Woman You Once Will Be

What will be left of gravity
and bone once the road this girl walks
opens skyward? She'll skid, vertiginous
to her toes (*how she loves*
that word), and if she floats
down a steep hill looking up?
You might, in the deep purple
jungle of your lungs, breathe out
a warning just loud enough
for her not to hear. Nobody
knows the rules.

She may get hurt. She may
sample riven rock,
break her teeth at the corner
or turn left, double back. She may
think hard about her circumstances
and change them, change
what she can in a cutting light softened
by a love she has felt, will feel
for the bone-deep beauty
of others on this road.

IV

Absence at Dusk

Hair gray, streaming, my mother
calls haltingly from half-way back
into the last century. She hovers just inches
above a precipice, the near dark stitching earth
to sky around her, the sound she makes
almost a song, almost articulate,
almost present. Just the other side of,
in between this
and that. Alongside the
first star visible.

Word Count: Sidewalk, Long Beach, Café Table

She appears—sudden, a reed-like
essence swaying over the vacant page
of your notebook. Hesitant, she says,

to interfere, but might you know
about writing, what inspires it? She's
post-menopausal, frankly warm

and she's lost her passion for things.
Perhaps you'd know, will
writing bring it back? Her blue bright

wide open eyes carry irritatingly
possible hope, her loping grace
driving her toward the precipice

of your unwritten sentence. She's
pressed her thumbprint on the scale
of wishes, your thoughts

scattered in bales of light
and burning water, dormant.
No hard science seeding this field.

Instead, a carapace muscled
to the body, brooding strategies
put aside so that one might just

accomplish utter stillness.
Shoot breath on the heat road,
thrum these little words

until—*melancholy*, she says.
Isn't that the old word for it?
Like a melody, of course,

an odd little sadness pooling
in crevices, in pillowing rock. You've
been melancholy yourself, thinking

of a child's luxury—timeless
urgent footprints of exploration
barefoot over sunny granite

on Long Island Sound, the sound
of flesh slapping rock
burned dry over the briny wash

the scrape of mollusks
a little girl, after all, safe
in the knowledge that the ones

who love her, love her,
until such time as she's old enough
to wonder about it all, and that's

melancholy, the old word for it—

This, these—words the delicate
scrollwork necessary to the ragged,
unfurling utterances of competent women

just slightly paused, at a loss for— you
must lift these words without touching,
a puff of air for the maneuver. Feather them

weightless toward her rumbling heart
to make a repair. You must
and will write soothing words,

for the life of you certain only
that one word curls into another
as this moment into that, and she

into you, and you into her
and this becomes a story.

Soul to Take

If I could palm it, what organ-
grinder's song would it sing
and to what pulse would it hiccup
a syllabic rendering of my name?

That sound you make, it's like
your father's, and maybe that's
his soul coming through you
and maybe that's how you get to
keep what he has, what he had

and so maybe I've got something
like that too, when I imagine the soul
damp in my hand, my dead father's
heart struggling to mouth my name
ill-equipped, as it is, for speaking.

What We Said About Limits

That more or less daily
the control we practice
is bunk. Laughable quantities
of good will and usefulness,
we said—squat! We were
cutting ourselves some slack,
taking a few hours, riding bikes
in the heat, dodging surly teenage boys
on skateboards who looked at us,
well, like we should fold up
and die instead of taking up another inch
of skateable asphalt, and although
it's true that we were just trying
to wear ourselves out so that we wouldn't
think too much more about how, not only
were we not going to save the world, but we
couldn't even save ourselves from our foolish
inabilities to help, I mean really help, our
ailing friend, it felt good, before it felt stupid
and awful, to look at those boys and think
about how they, too, if they were lucky
or maybe not, would grow old
and suffer, if they were not already,
in fact, suffering.

This Way of Being Here

As if the body were a thought removed
from itself. Free-floating. Baseless.
And yet still wanting what it wants
even when someone dies, to stretch
and bend, to sit at the counter for lunch,
to read the paper as if this
were normal, and it is.

When someone dies, this is a story
of what we do, bending into the thought,
the grief, the sheer loss saturating
the skin of being here, alive and separate.
Check the mirror for what it is that makes
these arms and legs move, the face
a puzzle of vanities, the *still here*
an echoing cave. When someone dies,

this is a story. The water closes
overhead, there's the impossible beyond,
a hapless figure, a shoreline,
minutes of fading light.

Before. After.

I hold her there, planting marigolds
across the footbridge each spring, taming her sorrow
in the front yard, although I never imagined
her sorrowful when I was that age, I mean
that age we lived before her husband died
with a suddenness, common as dirt, that
shook her like a rag.

Maybe I'm just making it up now,
that sorrow before the after, because now
she's been gone for fifty years, which is also
how long ago it was that men walked
on the moon, that her daughter graduated
from high school, that Woodstock, Charles Manson,
and the Moratorium to End the War in Vietnam happened,

and I think the way I think. It isn't
that she grows fainter. She's a stick figure
in that distance, lost mass the way I am losing mass,
but even if I can't quite hear her, or
know her beyond what was possible
for a seventeen-year-old to know,
I can feel it in my bones,
the weight she carries into this life
I've for so long had without her.

Late August from a Dead Stop

She's younger than me here, almost dying.
She needs a friend. She needs it all
to be different, but she won't say so.

I'd been dreaming words, a shuttlecock!
I'd woken hard to unsettle the house,
unearth and shed cups, glasses, bowls, plates,
unworn bracelets and rings, determined
to clear the decks for once, for all. Then
fell upon a multitude of ragged files

and found this letter I had never seen.
A voice I knew but could not claim
when I was seventeen, an adult writing
to adults. Composed, restrained, my mother
launched in widowhood lays down
into sentences the rasping notes of her days,
giving an account of herself to her in-laws,
her death looming. I see it ahead of her
though so far behind me now.

She's getting up each day
trying to move forward, her sorrow
so deep it threads an abeyance
of hope into my life, alongside
all that love. I hear her clearly now,
through the late August heat pressed
against me, her soft voice rising.

The Visit

1.

All over the universe
and from time to time
a sister wakes up
in her brother's house

her eyes opening
to the poses her young parents strike
in photographs he has hung
on the opposite wall.

On the windowsill, through which
emanates a dim but growing light,
she finds grandparents, aunts, uncles,
her first fish caught on a line.

Across the hall the brother
and sister-in-law stir in a sequence
of mornings that spin present life
into the fading, insistent past.

The sister, not quite warm enough
in her envelope of skin, wraps all this
around herself like a shawl and rises
in the old way. Shrugging her night fears

she steps into the blur of boundaries
that seem to gather, rather than separate,
who they were as children and what
they are now. Such is how

they live, strolling the shapely meadow
of time the visit offers them, surprised
by age, beloved, telling raucous stories
in full knowledge, in not knowing.

2.

A gentle tromp along the shore path
lunch with fish and rice and meat
a roundtable on the family foibles
then home to the hills where the house
settles into a busy quiet. One naps,
one works a list of chores, one settles
on the couch with a book in her lap.
A little reading, then the dropping back.

Sun paling, winter light in the ascending spring.
A bank of clouds, the bay, the great Pacific rim
all gather in this narrow neck of time,
this delicate flesh, this *us* still speaking.
We sort, arrange each day planted
in the flat world, willing ourselves
inward and up, fissuring the quotidian.

Slumber

The sun sank and rose, bracketing the night
and within it, the wee hour when
his breath gave out. Midsummer.

Remembered, as if yesterday. Everywhere
in the country the heat burned and whipped
the land, all but that strip of coast

so lovely and befogged, wrapped tight around us.
A hawk rose outside the window high up over the city
late that afternoon before the fall, sailing

the wind as if watching out for us. But maybe not.
Maybe the comfort is the hawk alive to its own efforts,
a force contiguous to my brother in his dying bed.

What comfort is there in the way time stops
but doesn't stop? He left while we were sleeping.
We woke to a trail gone cold.

V

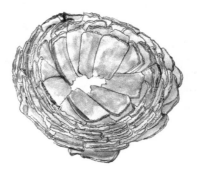

My Village

With its dirt-winding path grows little houses
like mushrooms after a spring rain. Easy
to see strolling by, they last
the length of time it takes to scythe
them down, the swift and elegant move
of a dispassionate hand.

Such is the rocky pasture of early evening. A mind
just hours ago paddling toward the riverbank path
that leads through pastel fields abundant with a soft
and satisfied wealth, now picks its pace
through a glimmering redness, burnt packages
of ideas that nevertheless court hope
in their rapid demise.

Ping Shan Heritage Trail, Hong Kong

The day overcast, the veil of brightening
gray sky over the northbound transit line promises
difference. Elegant towers of the city major
give way to panoramic fields sprouting projects
like teeth. A tourist, I feed myself into the mouth
of the New Territories, stepping from train to platform
to street pursuing clues to the Tang clan's ancestral past,
a walled village, a circular well overgrown
by a rush of pavement. Rural meets urban,
the guidebook says, a rapid mash.

I should understand this. A child of the past century
adrift in a landscape where blockish buildings
cut unforgiving angles into the sinuous horizon,
I should recognize progress when I see it.
Walking lost along the side of the road,
I look for remnants of a wall that once
protected the clan from invaders. They must have
poured across the fields, trampling the harvest
on their way toward rustling the livestock.

But this is neither here nor there.
Passing school children text into their phones,
a truck rolls by and I follow the curve of the road
toward the dwellings of the living. They might tell me
if I could only understand them, what it means
to pay homage to the dragon god whose benevolence
must ride the tendrils of air nipping the laundry
hung out to dry, the vegetable gardens, the quiet
of a late morning feathering an ancient wall.

Friday Morning

Even aloft in clear, chlorinated water
the muscles catch and grip each stroke this body—
lacking the fishiness of youth—must labor through,
pulling slow, reckoning breath that slips into
the keening weight of bones pledging the flesh
to some unpredictable current of decline.

The body cares about this, however, in the manner
of a young girl learning, for the first time, what it means
to take flight in water. Finding herself more than simply
adrift in her circumstances, she swoops and soars,
independent of helping hands, swimming hard toward
some unknown limit where she will meet herself.

A Figure

A gasp, nothing more. A dead rabbit
on the kitchen porch, half off the welcome mat,
and yet unwelcomed in the dash to get
the already drenched papers out of
the rain we have waited for
without much comment. We'd
been quiet, hoping we would not
have to rouse ourselves to water the great trees
too soon in a season of drought. Not even
summer yet, we'd think without saying,
gathering the papers crisp with news
we've sifted every morning in all the seasons
of our living together in this house, the pleasurable
companionship of this habit finally beginning to fade
under the persistence of bad news, repetitious news,
news that tells us nothing new about ourselves
because we are not thinking in that way
when we read it, we are not thinking, in fact,
much at all.

But a dead rabbit on the kitchen porch
in the pouring rain, bitten hard by something out there,
so that the blood staining the wooden planks is still fresh
enough to wash away even as the rabbit stiffens,
its head thrown back in some final agony I have not
yet experienced, that makes me think
the way a body can, through the clutch in the stomach
rather than through the mind. Several generations removed
from the days when skinning a dead rabbit was what you did,
I lean back into this day, having dealt with the problem,
alone in the house. This is neither
the end of civilization nor its beginning.
Nothing else is as clear.

When Brother Reckons

He leans through the window from outer space.
It's dark out there but the inside buttery light
glows in his hair, his head turning toward me. Only
the second, maybe the third, maybe fourth or fifth time
he's shown up in a dream. In the first, his bare torso
spun upward from murky waters, his limp body lighting
deep night, all that life-on-the-edge-of-death-ness
animating my sleep with sorrow, such that
I've not been able to pluck more visions
from the night road, until this

one moment of commentary: He reckons,
in his lightly conversant voice, how I ought
to be a better person. But wait, wait.

I can barely hear. He recedes behind the bank
of windows fronting the drifting house within which
I stake my claim to wakefulness, searching for the last word.

Virus Days, April

1.

I got nothing
to say about it.
The slow moat day
bristles supine.

Give me
succulence against
all this airy breath
settling in, room

to room across
my house. How
do we know
what we know?

2.

Under the super moon
every poem tacks its tail
on the poem before it, the donkey

you thought you loved until it
wandered off not
thinking of you

and then you
remembered you are not
the center.

You have never
lived this day before.
Three more caterpillars

on the Mexican butterfly
plant promise more Monarchs
if the weather holds

and if I
can fold myself into the
you I imagine here

something outside
this, what is it, skin?
Thing that leans out,

wishes a world wider
a you of me, a me spun
into darkling earth

3.

Brother & Me. Photograph:

Rosy baby blinking hard nosed
infatuated   / fragment of sister

to brother couplet, indefatigable piece
of one mind, peace wrought. Besieged

ascendant weariness trails. Years
ago now present, little fear

so easily aside, put. Older brother
next to, squats, talks. No other

necessary. A photograph
remembers what she, laughing,

cannot. A plague day renders
slow-moving hours, quirk

of thought, Brother. Step one, step two,
another step. What rhymes with you?

4.

Word count, April: 409 so far including
the days and their numbers.

At the big zoom meeting I plucked
my chin with tweezers, not knowing

my video was on. A decade ago
I might have cried out and cursed

but now all that just mumbles along
inside, like we do during a pandemic.

Not essential workers who make sure
all / all / all of us are fed and taken care of,

we stay home, offering a shrug
and a laugh to our colleagues

who have seen, now, just how human
we are. I sit under Miriam Beerman's

painting of a lizard catching a fly
and Rilke's *did you not know then,*

what joy is in reality, a terror
whose outcome we don't fear?

5.

Easter

Fear not, peasant,
I alone have come to etc.

Utterance fed to daylight
daylight fed to night. A bright

bloom of moonlight under which
Madame Defarge in the semblance

of my friend Karen makes masks to save
others from our corona droplets and ourselves

from torpor. Not, for heaven's sake,
that we imagine a French revolutionary

end point to the rows and rows of
minutes counted out for execution.

Not, I say. Should you want a moment
of feeling, a shiver of jouissance

find a river. Walk down through thickets
to its edge. Jump.

6.

April was here briefly. The breakwater visible, the lighthouse,
but no horizon.

—Carolyn Forché

Was there ever such a time? Always. Always.
The rarest of fields untouched by wrath or want—

right here, now, a thumbprint to the wind,
an ill-fitting hasp ground against the loop

of a closed, then padlocked trunk, its story
retold as if to the lasting benefit of all

who witnessed it. Emptied. We sit
and hope. We meander across the hot breath

of our citizenry. Some suffer. Others
do not suffer much. Some do not. This

to this and that to that. Plush fruit,
wilting vine, strong steps, halting, halting.

Who can count how many there are
behind each door, waiting?

7.

my gray zone
is starting to include poetry

here white is not absolute white
black is not absolute black
the edges of these non-colors
adjoin

—Tadeusz Rózewicz

The Mere Mention of Trains:

Distant romance or dread,
depending their uses.

Pennies on the track one
cold dawn in west Texas

silver frost-coated rails, yes!
A January, tilted toward unbridled

pleasure of horizon for us.
Citizens. My love. Outside

the night window, a whistle clack
of commerce draws other shadows:

a toddler sitting the shoulders of her father,
who walks the aisle of a train somewhere

in 1955, Pennsylvania, where
the forsythia must be blooming now.

We were so happy before we learned
the soundtrack of trains put to use

for darker purposes, unsettlingly human
waste and calculated rage. Cattle cars

of central Europe, torched trains of India,
children riding the Beast up the spine

of Mexico right now, trading death
for hope, hope for death. Yet a scrim

of happiness persists, no? Like
parallel rails, one never touching another

in the darkly lit pleasures of a night study
one hand on a book of poems, heart yearning,

horrified, hoping.

8.

Sylvia said she ate a light bulb
(she did not)

to put into practice this latest
promoted cure for the affliction

that haunts us. Bright sunlight bottled up
and swallowed whole, the president

must have thought, would sound good
to a lusting, beleaguered public.

I swore to myself he would not
be named, nor figure in any

April poem, yet here he is
while the people work and scrimp

and hunger and weep and laugh
and hope and save others and sometimes themselves

and phone home and keep in touch and sit
weeping or drooling or dreaming or working

hard, hard, harder against the endlessly
unfolding moment here,

here, here.

9.

The fathers of poetry
oh, the fathers of poetry beg
to be let alone while this situation
plays out. Ignoble present
tense itches and scratches
a rash that suddenly appears

on a chin once held
thoughtfully, in contemplation of
the infinite green of ponds dappled
with reeds and restless fish darting
here and there, a measure of time—

Must we ask where the mothers
of poetry linger? Have we not
gotten there ourselves, dipped
in the skirting necessity to sister
and brother and mother in a
cartoon bundle of whirling legs

and arms? We love, fitful.
We are aware of falling short.
We are thankful for distracting
rain, bird call, wild life returning
to the cities we have neglected,
our intelligent hearts failing.

Inside the Loop

Distance from Houston to the border, circa 350 miles
Distance from house to work, circa 5 miles
Distance from Brownsville to Falfurrias, circa 127 miles
Distance to the neighbor's house where they are drinking
mint juleps and betting on the Kentucky Derby,
maybe 2 tenths of a mile—distance. A body at rest,
having taken circa 12 thousand steps in good shoes,
sits at a desk, clothed appropriately.

Distance from Houston to Mexico City, 752 miles. Flight time
2 hours 30, give or take. Time to hotel maybe 30 minutes
unless she goes Metro, and then, it depends. She faces
an unfamiliar crush of people, frightened by the heave
of bodies, the sense of being lifted off her feet,
then outraged by the man who, face to face, averts his eyes
but not the hands groping for the zippers on her bag. Later,
she will have a good time anyway, having saved her stuff.
Once she gets settled, once she finds something to eat.

An unfamiliar crush. Dots on a map in the *Times*
mark human remains between Brownsville and Falfurrias,
trafficked out past the fields of sunflowers she saw once,
driving Rte. 281 to the border. She remembers snippets,
Falfurrias butter, the dairy ranch family whose wealth
and progressivist efforts in early 20th century Texas
she heard bits about from the philanthropic descendants
she knew once, while she was studying Américo Paredes
on tejanos and the rinche/rangers in South Texas.
So she would know her country, its injustices,
and what it takes to keep a sense of humor
through hard times. Her country. Not her country.

Alone in the house, at a distance. Her country
in the nearest photograph, a 6-year-old brother
squatting next to his baby sister in her chair, telling her things,
central Pennsylvania, 1952. He could still squat like that,
telling her things, at 67, but the healthy, happy baby girl?
No squatting, not for years. Where he is buried, she can hear
the shouts from the schoolyard across the way,
children playing in the intervals between classes.
Beyond that, circa 3 miles, the Pacific Ocean.
A hawk, quail, a bobcat, an owl.

Distance from Houston to Mill Valley, circa 1,941 miles.
Distance from the grave to the water?

Even now, people walk, fall, rise. They try
to save themselves or one another, utter a prayer,
a curse. One kills something or someone off.
Another stands still. Falls down. The world passes
from their lives.

Sometimes in the distance she can see
the hazy the outlines of the Marin Headlands.
She is either visiting, looking northwest
from the Oakland hills, or she is watching television
in Houston, when a sudden shot of San Francisco Bay
flips by. She thinks the mountains at some point will slip
into the sea. Several valleys up the coast
his human remains will tumble along with them
but she will not know it, nor where her remains will be.

A body afloat, unknown in a river of newsprint
that flows from distant headwaters. Massacred figures
made ready in their shrouds to be lifted, then lowered
(or dropped) according to either custom or circumstance
in another country. That place, those places. She remembers

the gasp, the swift, almost silent uptake of breath
when the body of her brother was lifted from the hearse
wrapped in the shroud they chose because there would be
no box no chemical no make-up no bronze vault no distance
from earth, from dirt. His head dropped because this was not
newsprint and there was no photograph, no metaphor to make
still or distant the idea of his death. His wife and she and all
those gathered would take the shovels themselves
and bury him.

Distance. A flight of birds thwarted by cataclysm.
In damp heat, a bayou overrunning its banks. Flood
upon flood of unfolding story. They will take their shovels.

July Ides / A Ghazal

Something recollected under clear and present weather
spins currents, dust clouds spilling under the weather.

Barefoot late afternoon blistering porch boards
you can't stand still for. Under the weather

a poisonous rupture midpoint. You'd been doing well.
plump sleep, satisfied waking, hunger under the weather—

just don't tell me you're fine. Fine. Come on in.
Dive down, the old dirt cellar door open. Under the weather

an empty coal scuttle, dim remembered shapes flank
stone walls, a perfect place to hide under the weather.

If we could only live in the past! You've thought it,
shamed to admit. That old dreamt house under the weather

storms the mind, an irreducible loss and therefore limitless,
perfect, a stone-dropped ripple, radiant under the weather.

Old elegant sorrows blanket time, the present sucked flat
when you act this way, shriveling yourself under weather

instead of bending toward the light—if frightening—touch
of the near world passing and breaking into this weather.

Where do you think you live? Faint bellowing mist
permeates gathering crowds. Under the weather

they dart and slide beside themselves, clap hands.
Don't stifle yourself. Slip your fingers under the weather

and lift the slippery, drifting weight, Jane, the choir of infinite
mortal cells carrying all, all of us, under the weather.

Here and There

At the edge of blank reverie, there will always
be a field in sunlight, edged by woods, floating
several hills up from home, from the broken sidewalk
and grass of the first toddling footfalls that grew
in a few short years to running bursts across that field.

For each of us a field, a stoop, a street, a desert trail,
a box canyon, or concrete, concrete, concrete, a patch
of grass, all various and recognizable, the shaping places
before there was "before," before we knew the dam
could be built or the dam could burst and our landscapes
would all change, no matter what of them we carried with us.

In my field, a brother and a father walk alongside.
We are separate and together, each of us
finding our way in the company of the others,
and because of this, I know how to find my way
through uncertainties, no matter how long it takes.

Supplicant

Let me have the love it takes
to live inside this dream where you
and you and you and you are walking
a road. It leads down to a lake
I know, banked by granite boulders
and pine, and I am also with you
and you and you and you walking
one by one and together, as if
we had all, always, been friends
who loved one another
in the same place, at the same time.

ACKNOWLEDGMENTS

"Where There Is No Else" appeared in *Enchantment of the Ordinary*, Guest Editor John Gorman, Mutabilis Press, 2018.

"The Trees on Prairie Road" appeared in *Texas Poetry Calendar 2021*, Editor Jeanie Sanders, Kallisto Gaia Press.

NOTES

"The Afternoon is the Medium" was inspired by Aditi Machado's "Then," originally published in *Poem-a-Day* on December 14, 2020, by the Academy of American Poets.

The epigraph to section 6 of "Virus Days, April" comes from the poem "The Angel of History," Part I in *The Angel of History* by Carolyn Forché, HarperPerennial, 1994.

The epigraph to section 7 of "Virus Days, April" comes from the poem "gray zone," in *New Poems* by Tadeusz Różewicz, translated from the Polish by Bill Johnston, Archipelago Books, 2007.

GRATITUDE

I am thankful beyond measure for Karen Latuchie, whose love and friendship have made these poems possible, and for Robin Reagler, who walked alongside me to usher so many of them into daylight.

My gratitude to Pat Jasper, Harriet Barlow, and Wendy Watriss for friendships across a lifetime that have given shape and vision to this road we're traveling. I am grateful for the steadfast love of Susan Plunkett and Sylvia Gasoi, first experienced several decades ago in the streets and wild kitchens of Rochester, New York. Thank you to Angel Quesada and Alicia Kahn, who together introduced me to the haunting beauty of *Florisphaera profunda* and wrapped that beauty around this book.

Thank you to Blue Mountain Center and Tyrone Guthrie Centre at Annaghmakerrig, where some of these poems were seeded and written. Thank you to Robin Davidson for recommending me to Saint Julian Press, and to Ron Starbuck for the faith and stamina to create and run such a beautiful enterprise in poetry.

This book exists in great part because I had a brother, Allan Creighton, who—before I could even put words together—struck up a conversation with me about this world and what we might do in it. The radiant sound of his voice still and always with us, I am grateful for my beloved sister, Ann Tracy, my sister-in-law, Julie Nesnansky, our brilliant nephews and nieces—Michael Tracy and Joslyn Nolasco, Tara Tracy and Grant Kauwe, and all the conversation yet to come.

And finally, I am thankful beyond measure for Jim Blain, who shares this life with me.

ABOUT THE AUTHOR

Jane Creighton is a poet, essayist, and Professor of English at the University of Houston—Downtown, where she teaches literature and creative writing. A recipient of a Fulbright Fellowship, she taught American literature for a year at Jagiellonian University in Kraków, Poland. In the decades prior to her university teaching, her social activism included holding organizing positions with the National Lawyers Guild and the Center for Constitutional Rights. In the 1970s, she edited and published an independent poetry magazine, *Sailing the Road Clear*, and in subsequent years taught writing in public schools for the Texas Commission on the Arts, Teachers & Writers Collaborative, and Writers in the Schools. In 1987, she served as literary curator for the Washington Project on the Arts exhibition, *War and Memory in the Aftermath of Vietnam*. Her publications include *Ploughshares*, *Gulf Coast*, *Poetry Foundation*, *Enchantment of the Ordinary*, *We Begin Here: Poems for Palestine and Lebanon*, *Unwinding the Vietnam War*, *Close to the Bone: Memoirs of Hurt, Rage, and Desire*, *Encountering Disgrace: Reading and Teaching Coetzee's Novel*, and *Still Seeking an Attitude: Critical Reflections on the Work of June Jordan*. She is the author of an early collection of poems, *Ceres in an Open Field*. Originally from the northeast, she has lived in Houston for thirty-three years.

Typefaces Used:

TYPEFACE: PERPETUA TILTING MT
TYPEFACE: GARAMOND – Garamond

CPSIA information can be obtained
at www.ICGtesting.com
Printed in the USA
BVHW030945280821
615448BV00007B/229